ALLOSAURUS

BY REBECCA SABELKO

BELLWETHER MEDIA · MINNEAPOLIS, MN

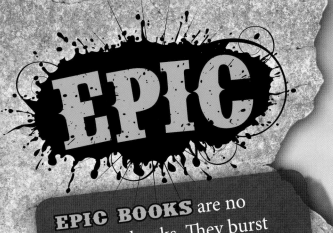

EPIC BOOKS are no ordinary books. They burst with intense action, high-speed heroics, and shadows of the unknown. Are you ready for an Epic adventure?

This edition first published in 2021 by Bellwether Media, Inc.

No part of this publication may be reproduced in whole or in part without written permission of the publisher. For information regarding permission, write to Bellwether Media, Inc., Attention: Permissions Department, 6012 Blue Circle Drive, Minnetonka, MN 55343.

Library of Congress Cataloging-in-Publication Data

Names: Sabelko, Rebecca, author.
Title: Allosaurus / Rebecca Sabelko.
Description: Minneapolis, MN : Bellwether Media, 2021. | Series: Epic : The world of dinosaurs |
Includes bibliographical references and index. | Audience: Ages 7-12 | Audience: Grades 4-6 |
Summary: "Engaging images accompany information about the allosaurus. The combination of high-interest subject matter and light text is intended for students in grades 2 through 7"-- Provided by publisher.
Identifiers: LCCN 2020014863 (print) | LCCN 2020014864 (ebook) |
ISBN 9781644872901 (library binding) | ISBN 9781681038353 (paperback) |
ISBN 9781681037530 (ebook)
Subjects: LCSH: Allosaurus--Juvenile literature.
Classification: LCC QE862.S3 S23223 2021 (print) | LCC QE862.S3 (ebook) | DDC 567.912--dc23
LC record available at https://lccn.loc.gov/2020014863
LC ebook record available at https://lccn.loc.gov/2020014864

Editor: Betsy Rathburn   Designer: Jeffrey Kollock

Printed in the United States of America, North Mankato, MN

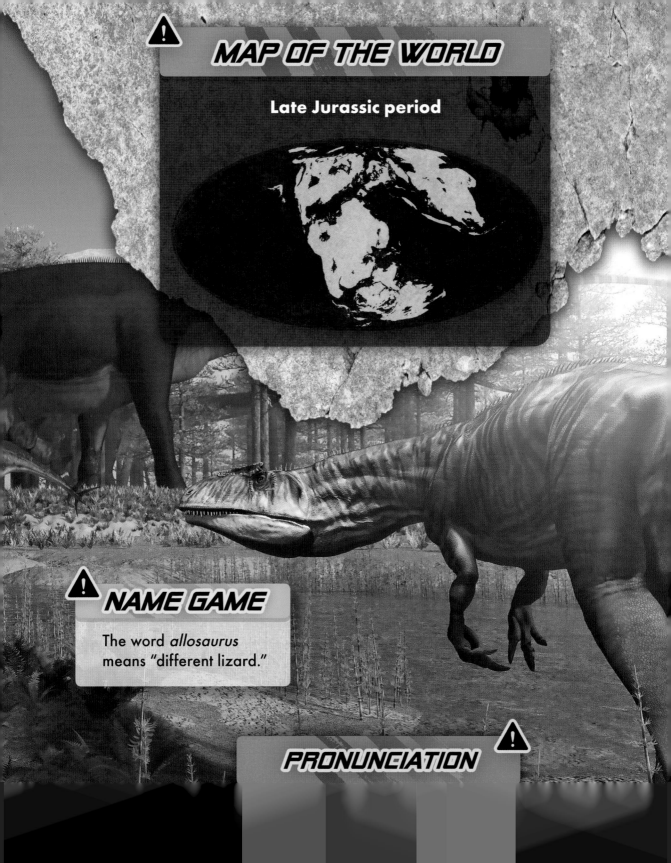

MAP OF THE WORLD

Late Jurassic period

NAME GAME

The word *allosaurus* means "different lizard."

PRONUNCIATION

WHAT WAS THE ALLOSAURUS?

horn

claw

The allosaurus was a large dinosaur. It grew up to 17 feet (5 meters) tall!
It had a large head with horns above its eyes. Its short arms ended in sharp, hooked claws.

⚠ MYSTERY HORNS

Scientists are not sure why this dinosaur had horns. Some believe the horns were used in battles!

⚠ SIZE CHART

15 feet (4.6 meters)

10 feet (3 meters)

5 feet (1.5 meters)

This dinosaur was a **theropod**. It walked on two powerful legs. These helped the dinosaur run faster than its **prey**.

Its tail was long and stiff. It helped the dinosaur balance on its two legs.

TOP SPEED

The allosaurus could run more than 20 miles (32 kilometers) per hour!

DIET AND DEFENSES

⚠ YOUNG MEAT

Allosaurus young may have become prey to hungry adults.

The allosaurus was an **apex predator**. It often hunted large plant eaters.

Allosaurus prey was strong and dangerous. The allosaurus may have hunted in groups to take down larger prey!

ALLOSAURUS DIET

stegosaurus

camptosaurus

diplodocus

NEW TEETH

The allosaurus's teeth often became dull. Dull teeth were replaced by new, sharper teeth!

The allosaurus had a wide jaw full of teeth. It ran at prey with an open mouth. Its upper teeth sank into its prey. Slashing bites helped the dinosaur rip out chunks of meat!

The allosaurus weakened its prey with a strong bite. Its hooked claws likely held down prey. Then the dinosaur finished its meal.

The allosaurus could not chew.
It swallowed entire mouthfuls of meat!

young
allosaurus

FOSSILS AND EXTINCTION

Earth's **climate** began to change near the end of the Jurassic period. Life began to **evolve**, too.

The allosaurus could not survive the changes. It went **extinct**.

The first allosaurus **fossil** was found in the late 1800s in the western United States. Many more have been found since.

BIG AL

Scientists discovered a nearly complete allosaurus skeleton in 1991. They named it Big Al.

ALLOSAURUS FOSSIL MAP

North America

Europe

Africa

South America

KEY

fossil site

New discoveries teach us more about the mighty allosaurus!

GET TO KNOW THE ALLOSAURUS

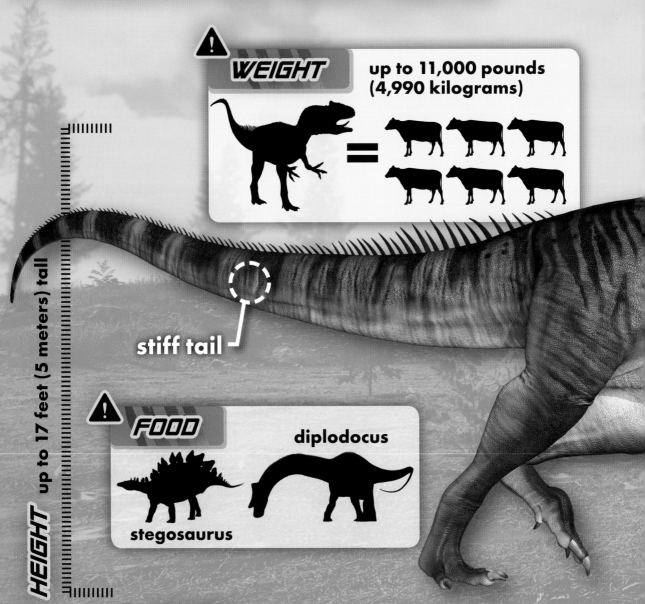

⚠️ **WEIGHT** up to 11,000 pounds (4,990 kilograms)

=

stiff tail

⚠️ **FOOD**

stegosaurus

diplodocus

HEIGHT up to 17 feet (5 meters) tall

LENGTH up to 39 feet (12 meters) long

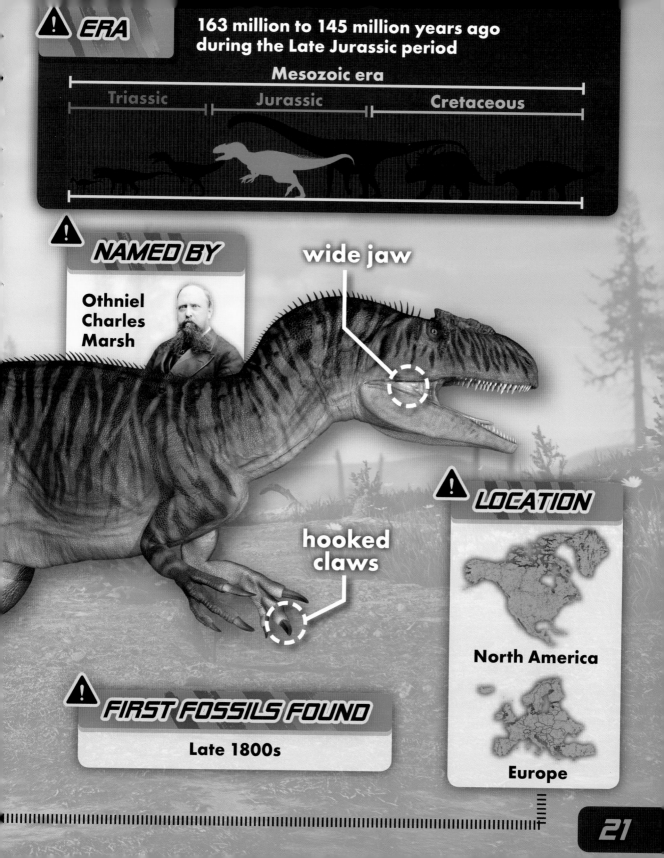

⚠ ERA

163 million to 145 million years ago during the Late Jurassic period

Mesozoic era

Triassic | Jurassic | Cretaceous

⚠ NAMED BY

Othniel Charles Marsh

wide jaw

⚠ LOCATION

hooked claws

North America

Europe

⚠ FIRST FOSSILS FOUND

Late 1800s

GLOSSARY

apex predator—an animal at the top of the food chain; apex predators are not preyed upon by any other animals.

climate—the usual weather in a certain area over long periods of time

evolve—to change slowly, often into a better, more complex state

extinct—no longer living

fierce—strong and dangerous

fossil—a remnant of something that lived long ago

Jurassic period—the second period of the Mesozoic era that occurred between 200 million and 145 million years ago; the Late Jurassic period began around 163 million years ago.

Mesozoic era—a time in history in which dinosaurs lived on Earth; the first birds, mammals, and flowering plants appeared on Earth during the Mesozoic era.

prey—animals hunted by other animals for food

theropod—a meat-eating dinosaur that had two small arms and moved on two legs

TO LEARN MORE

AT THE LIBRARY

Doeden, Matt. *Could You Survive the Jurassic Period?: An Interactive Prehistoric Adventure*. North Mankato, Minn.: Capstone Press, 2020.

Pimentel, Annette Bay. *Do You Really Want to Meet Allosaurus?* Mankato, Minn.: Amicus Ink, 2020.

Suen, Anastasia. *Allosaurus*. Vero Beach, Fla.: Rourke Educational Media, 2019.

ON THE WEB

FACTSURFER

Factsurfer.com gives you a safe, fun way to find more information.

1. Go to www.factsurfer.com.

2. Enter "allosaurus" into the search box and click 🔍.

3. Select your book cover to see a list of related content.

INDEX

The images in this book are reproduced through the courtesy of: James Kuether, front cover, pp. 4-5, 6-7, 8-9, 10-11, 12-13, 14-15, 16-17, 20-21; Herschel Hoffmeyer, p. 11 (stegosaurus); Warpaint, p. 11 (diplodocus, camptosaurus); EQRoy, pp. 18, 19; Wikipedia, p. 21 (Othniel Charles Marsh).